YOU BE GOOD & I'LL BE NIGHT

JUMP·ON·THE·BED POEMS

YOU BE GOOD & I'LL BE NIGHT

Eve Merriam

PICTURES BY KAREN LEE SCHMIDT

A MULBERRY PAPERBACK BOOK

NEW YORK

The Library of Congress has cataloged the Morrow Junior Books
edition of *You Be Good and I'll Be Night* as follows:
Merriam, Eve, 1916–1992
You be good and I'll be night; jump-on-the-bed poems
Summary: Thirty-five pages of brief rhyming poems.
ISBN 0-688-06742-5   ISBN 0-688-06743-3 (lib. bdg.)
1. Children's poetry, American. [1. American poetry]
I. Schmidt, Karen Lee, ill. II. Title.
PS3525.E639Y68 1988 811'.54 87-24859
First Mulberry Edition, 1994.
ISBN 0-688-13984-1

F O R

Hannah

You be saucer,
I'll be cup,
piggyback, piggyback,
pick me up.

You be tree,
I'll be pears,
carry me, carry me
up the stairs.

You be Good,
I'll be Night,
tuck me in, tuck me in
nice and tight. ✧

Hop on one foot,
jump with two,
skip, skip,
where's my shoe?

Skip in a circle,
skip in a square,
lost my shoe,
don't know where.

Jump on the bed,
lump inside:
here's my shoe
trying to hide. ✧

Crusty corn bread,
crumbly crumbs,
mumbly muffins,
buttery thumbs.

Flaky biscuits,
crunchy toast,
cracks in the crackers
crumble the most. ✧

I know a boy,
I know a girl,
whirligig whirligig whirligig whirl.

The girl is Pearl,
the boy is Roy,
hobbledy hobbledy hobbledy hoy.

Roy's sister is Joy,
Pearl's brother is Earl,
whirligig whirligig whirligig whirl.

And I am me
and you are you,
whirligig whirligig hobbledy hoo. ✧

I found a little stone
round as the moon,
my own little stone
smooth as a spoon.

I keep my little stone
in a water jar,
it shines dark as night
without any star. ✧

Ghosty ghosty all alone,
can't talk on the telephone.

Ghosty ghosty groany groan,
drops his chocolate ice cream cone.

Ghosty ghosty moany moan,
lost the wish from the chicken bone.

Ghosty ghosty all alone,
needs a ghosty of his own. ✧

Swing me, swing me, swing me round,
I don't want my feet to touch the ground.

Swing me an hour, swing me some more,
swing me until a quarter past four.

Swing me till summer, swing me through fall,
I promise I'll never get tired at all. ✧

Jump, jump,
jump in the ring,
jump, jump,
what will you bring?

You bring a door with double locks,
I'll bring a pair of cotton socks.

You bring a house made of building blocks,
I'll bring a dozen cuckoo clocks.

You bring a boat that's down at the docks,
I'll bring an engine that knocks knocks knocks.

You bring chickens and hens and cocks,
I'll bring shepherds and all their flocks,
and we'll put them all in a GREAT BIG BOX. ✧

Sheep, sheep, sleeps in a fold,
warm and woolly against the cold.

Bird, bird, sleeps in the sky,
up in a nest cradled on high.

Bear, bear, in a cozy den,
sleeps till springtime comes again.

Caterpillar in a silky cocoon
wakes as a butterfly soon, soon. ✧

Hello, hello,
who's calling, please?

> Mr. Macaroni
> and a piece of cheese.

Hello, hello,
hello, who's there?

> Honey Buzzbee
> and a big brown bear.

Hello, hello,
will you spell your name?

> It's R.A.T.
> and yours is the same.

Hello, hello,
what did you say?

> The rain is over,
> let's go out and play. ✧

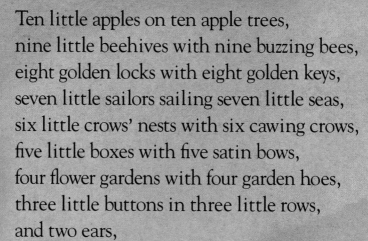

Ten little apples on ten apple trees,
nine little beehives with nine buzzing bees,
eight golden locks with eight golden keys,
seven little sailors sailing seven little seas,
six little crows' nests with six cawing crows,
five little boxes with five satin bows,
four flower gardens with four garden hoes,
three little buttons in three little rows,
and two ears,
two eyes,
one mouth,
and a nose. ✧

Fish, fish,
make a wish.

I wish for a river
that runs to the sea,
I wish to nest in
a coral tree.

I long for the darkness
below the light foam,
I long for the ocean,
I wish to be home. ✧

In the woods,
deep down damp,
piggy feet stop,
piggy feet stamp.

Waddle
snuffle
dig dig dig
piggety piggety
piggety pig.✧

Hunter on the horse, fox on the run,
train leaves the station at one oh one.

Buckle on the belt, lace in the shoe,
train leaves the station at two oh two.

Worm in the garden, apple on the tree,
train leaves the station at three oh three.

Light on the ceiling, rug on the floor,
train leaves the station at four oh four.

Berry on the bush, honey in the hive,
train leaves the station at five oh five.

Salt in the ocean, clay in the bricks,
train leaves the station at six oh six.

Snake in the grass, angel in heaven,
train leaves the station at seven oh seven.

Ink in the pen, chalk on the slate,
train leaves the station at eight oh eight.

Sand in the desert, coal in the mine,
train leaves the station at nine oh nine.

Cow in the barn, bear in the den,
train got stuck at the station again. ✧

Pins and needles,
thread and buttons,
hooks and a snap.

Mommy sews
while cat takes a nap.

Pins and needles,
thread and buttons,
hooks and a snap.

Up jumps cat
like a thunderclap:

Nins and peedles,
bread and thuttons,
snooks and a hap. ✧

Harriet, by magic force,
turned herself into a horse.
Combed her pretty ponytail,
ate her dinner from a pail,
snorted water from a trough,
and never took her horseshoes off. ✧

Violet picks bluebells,
bakes blueberry pies,
whistles like a blue jay,
catches bluebottle flies.

Violet's eyes are bluest blue,
and she stays in swimming
till her lips are, too. ✧

Lunch box, lunch box,
what's for lunch?
Peanut butter sandwich
and celery to crunch,
carrots and banana
and an apple to munch.
A bite and a bite
and a *bite* and a BITE,
now I'm heavy
and my lunch box is light. ✧

Wind takes the world
and gives it a whoop,
wind gathers leaves
like a giant scoop.

Wind whips sails
and makes them clap,
wind knocks my head
clear out of my cap.

Wind rattles floorboards
and makes them sigh,
but kites take the wind
and fly fly fly. ✧

Snow in the east,
snow in the west,
snow on my eyelashes
I like best.

Grass in the east,
grass in the west,
grass on my knee bones
I like best.

Rain in the east,
rain in the west,
rain on my bare feet
I like best.

Light in the east,
light in the west,
light in my window
I like best.

Night in the east,
night in the west,
night in my own bed
I like best. ✧

Tabby on the prowl,
Tabby at the tap,
Tabby in a bureau drawer,
Tabby in a lap.

Tabby at a saucer
lapping milk,
Tabby cleaning whiskers
smooth as silk.

Tabby leaping fences,
Tabby up a tree,
Tabby stretching to the moon
and jumping down to me. ✧

Knobby green pickle,
wrinkled purple prune,
what can you see
by the light of the moon?

Silver satin pickle,
velvet silver prune,
everything changes
in the light of the moon. ✧

You're my turtle,
you're my dove,
coo, coo,
you're the one I love.

You're my safety,
you're my pin,
hold me close
and fasten me in.

You're my jumping,
you're my jack,
wherever you go,
you always come back. ✧

Guess what I've got inside my fist—
a snowflake that melted,
a hug that ran away,
and a kiss that's waiting to be kissed. ✧

Cold cold shivery cold me in
warm warm warm blanket rolled me in
hold hold old teddy bear hold me in
story story storytime told me in
night night warm darkness fold me in
sun sun morning sun gold me in. ✧